THOMAS CRANE PUBLIC LIBRARY
QUINCY MASS
CITY APPROPRIATION

Future Transport
ON WATER

By Steve Parker
Illustrations by David West

 Marshall Cavendish
Benchmark

New York

This edition first published in 2012 in the United States by
Marshall Cavendish Benchmark

An imprint of Marshall Cavendish Corporation

Website: www.marshallcavendish.us

This publication represents the opinions and views of the author based on Steve Parker's personal experience, knowledge, and research. The information in this book serves as a general guide only. The author and publisher have used their best efforts in preparing this book, and disclaim liability rising directly and indirectly from the use and application of this book.

Other Marshall Cavendish Offices:
Marshall Cavendish International (Asia) Private Limited, 1 New Industrial Road, Singapore 536196 • Marshall Cavendish International (Thailand) Co Ltd. 253 Asoke, 12th Flr, Sukhumvit 21 Road, Klongtoey Nua, Wattana, Bangkok 10110, Thailand • Marshall Cavendish (Malaysia) Sdn Bhd, Times Subang, Lot 46, Subang Hi-Tech Industrial Park, Batu Tiga, 40000 Shah Alam, Selangor Darul Ehsan, Malaysia

Marshall Cavendish is a trademark of Times Publishing Limited

Library of Congress Cataloging-in-Publication Data

Parker, Steve, 1952-
On water / Steve Parker.
p. cm. -- (Future transport)
Includes bibliographical references and index.
Summary: "Gives a concise history of travel by land, water, air, or in space, showing the technology available today, in the near future, and in centuries to come"--Provided by publisher.
ISBN 978-1-60870-780-5 (print)
1. Ships--Juvenile literature. 2. Boats and boating--Juvenile literature. 3. Ocean travel--Juvenile literature. I. Title. II. Series.

VM150.P3474 2012
387.2--dc22

2011001129

Produced by
David West 🏃 Children's Books
7 Princeton Court
55 Felsham Road
London SW15 1AZ

Designer: Gary Jeffrey
Illustrator: David West

The photographs in this book are used by permission and through the courtesy of:
Abbreviations: t-top, m-middle, b-bottom, r-right, l-left, c-center.
title page, 30m, PSA/fotoseeker.com; 6-7, Kroisenbrunner; 7ml, Dennis Ingemansson, 7tr, US Navy; 8l, Cruise News Weekly, 8b, Baldwin040; 9t, 9r, Cygnus Co. ©, 9m, America World City, 9bl, angermann; 10t, Etan Tal, 10l, VollwertBIT, 10b, 21tl, Austal Ships; 11t, 17b, Solar Sailor Holdings Ltd, 11ml, Elke Seemann, 11mr, Commercial Naval Architects Pty Ltd, 11b, Marine Advanced Reasearch, Inc.; 12t, Det Norske Veritas, 12l, SkySails GmbH & Co. KG., 12r, SteKrueBe; 13t, Siemens AG, 13ml, Wallenius Wilhelmsen Logistics, 13b, Ulstein Group ASA; 14m, Guillermo Sureda Burgos, 14b, HAWC Technologies LLC; 15t, Bachcell, 15m, AirLift Hovercraft; 16tl, Green Jet yacht (by Erik Sifrer, Mides design, Slovenia), 16tr, WHY; 17t, Bavaria Yachtbau GmbH, 17m, SABDES Design www.sabdes.com, 17ml, David Castor; 18t, Maritime Flight Dnamics inc, 18bl, Greg Kolodziejzyk, 18m, David Pearlman. U-Boat Worx B.V., 18r, Gibbs Technologies, Inc.; 19b, Nikko Van Stolk; 20t, 20b, 26tl, U.S Navy, 20m, 21bl, United States Navy, John F. Williams; 21r, U.S. Navy photo by Mass Communication Specialist 2nd Class Kristopher Wilson, 21br, Xiziz, 22t, 23t, NOAA, 22m, BAE Systems, 22, bl, Marion Hyper-Submersible Powerboat Design, LLC/www.hyper-sub.com, 22br, U-Boat Worx B.V.; 24t, Kim Hoffman, 24l, Sandstein, 24b, uscg; 25l, Griffon Hoverwork, 25r, Coast Guard photo by Petty Officer 3rd Class Connie Terrell; 26t, NASA, 26tr, PR_Radnomade_Project_MCS, 26b, Mike Baird; 26tr, STX Europe in collaboration with SDI, 26m, Robert Allan Ltd, 26b, Joe Schneid, Louisville, Kentucky; 28r, williamcho, 28b, Cameron Lyall; 29tr, Zaha Hadid Architects, 29b, Zigloo; 30t, Lila-Lou Yacht Design

Printed in China
135642

Contents

INTRODUCTION

"Seaport Five is pleased to offer the following attractions on this warm, sunny morning. We have freestyle jetskiing, mini-submarine races, a buried treasure search, and the ever-popular solar-powered scuba challenge. Have a great time. And always remember—water is your friend!"

We love to have fun in water. For centuries people have paddled, swam, and sailed. Now we snorkel, surf, windsurf, kitesurf, paraglide, waterski, scuba-dive, and powerboat. Will the future see new games and sports among the waves?

More importantly for the whole world, will we see more travel and transport by water? New inventions and ever-better technology for passenger ships, ferries, and cargo-carriers could ease problems such as global warming, human overcrowding, pollution, and dwindling energy resources.

HISTORY OF WATERCRAFT

Water is the oldest form of large-scale transport. More than 20,000 years ago, people paddled simple log rafts. By 5,000 years ago sailing ships captured the wind.

The trireme galley combined oars and sails and was used by Phoenicians, Greeks, Romans, and many other peoples.

SEA TRADE

As people explored the ancient world, their sailing ships became faster and better at using wind energy. From the Phoenicians, 3,500 years ago, to the Venetians in the eighth to eighteenth centuries, people built empires by trading across the seas. Exotic goods, brought from afar, made vast fortunes.

Clippers in the nineteenth century brought precious cargo to rich markets.

One of the smallest, simplest watercraft is the coracle, in use over 2,000 years ago in western Britain and Ireland. Waterproofed animal skins cover its willow frame.

Singapore's Keppel Container Terminal is a world trading center.

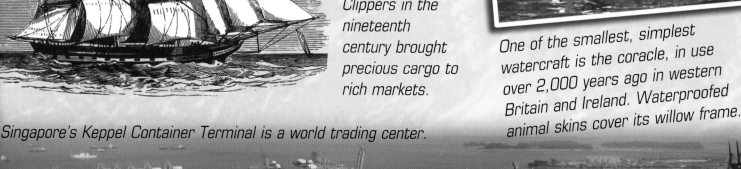

NAVAL POWER

Many conflicts have turned on famous sea battles, from the Punic Wars between Rome and Carthage 2,200 years ago, to the epic naval clashes of World War II (1939–1945). Today the greatest vessels afloat represent both trade and military power, and leisure, with vast crude-oil tankers, giant warships, and huge luxury cruise liners.

The struggle to rule the seas led navies to develop new inventions, from the hydrofoil (above) to the submarine.

One U.S. Nimitz class aircraft supercarrier has more weaponry and fighting power than some small countries.

Technology that we can hardly imagine, such as spinning motors that produce a hovering effect over water, could power craft of the future.

"Seemed like a good idea..."

In 1947 the Kon Tiki raft expedition tried to show that people reached the Pacific islands by drifting west from South America. Modern evidence shows they probably came east from Asia.

Go Cruising

Before long-haul air travel took off in the 1950s, travelers spent weeks at sea on great ocean liners. Future liners are less for going from A to B, as for luxury tourism.

In contrast to its younger sister ship Titanic, Olympic had a long and successful career from 1911 to 1935.

Queens of the Seas

One of the most famous liners was *Titanic*, tragically sunk by an iceberg collision in 1912.

In 2004 Queen Mary 2 led the new trend for massive luxury liners. Just a few years later, plans are being made for vessels twice as big.

At 52,000 tons (47,000 t), *Titanic* carried 3,500 people. Yet that is one-quarter the weight and one-half the passengers of the newest mega-cruisers, which offer the very best in food, drink, leisure, and places to visit.

At 225,000 tons (204,000 t), Oasis of the Seas is one of the largest vessels afloat. Over 6,000 passengers can enjoy its central park area (far left).

A cruiser takes more than ten years from plans to passengers. Here Queen Elizabeth 2 is equipped with fittings including a vast main staircase (below).

Limits on Size

Can cruise liners keep growing? There are limits such as the depth of water in ports, and the width of harbor entrances and canals. But on the open ocean, bigger is better— and in some ways safer. Huge ships are more stable in high winds and tall waves.

In another twenty-five years, liners could carry 10,000 travelers. But the cruise business depends on rich people. If world finances fall into bad recession, liners could be mothballed or even scrapped.

"Seemed like a good idea…"

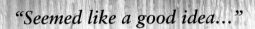

One of the great attractions of cruising is "taking the sea air" on the promenade deck. In the 1930s, Norman Bel Geddes and his designers forgot this and proposed to keep all passengers behind glass. The totally enclosed ocean liner was never built.

How Stabilizers Work

Many large vessels have some kind of dampers or stabilizers along the sides, under the waterline. The large surface area of these fin-shaped devices helps to reduce side-to-side rolling. Some stabilizers have added propellers or waterjets.

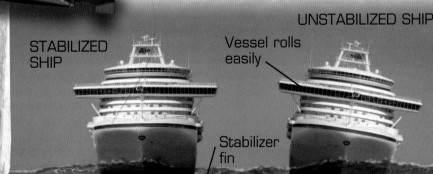

UNSTABILIZED SHIP

STABILIZED SHIP

Vessel rolls easily

Stabilizer fin

FUTURE FERRIES

Hard-working ferries are not so glamorous. They carry people and freight to and fro, non-stop, in all weathers. But fresh ideas could make these workhorses safer, more efficient, and even more fun!

Typical RoRo ferries, here in Turkey, have strict schedules to keep. On short routes, load-unload periods take up more than two-thirds of working time.

Norway's Color Line craft are at sea for twenty-four hours or more, with 700 cars and 2,500 passengers. Ferry companies compete for speed, comfort, and price.

Austal make several kinds of high-speed catamaran and trimaran ferries. Each one is tested during sea trials, as shown here, to make sure all systems are working and safe for relentless public use.

Roll On, Roll Off

"RoRo" ferries carry cars, trucks, and other vehicles which can roll on and off. They began in the 1950s, and soon several ramps at the bow (front), stern (rear), and side speeded up drive-thru loading and unloading. Planned RoRo ferries will hold over 8,000 cars and have adjustable decks if they need to take tall trucks.

Solar panels double as sails

Diesel engine and rechargeable batteries in hull

SolarSailor

One of a series of ferries for across-harbor trips, SolarSailor is a hybrid of electrical and diesel power plus wind propulsion. Its fold-out solar panels work as sails.

Going Green

Clear skies are more common over the sea than above many places on land. Also fuel is a huge part of a ferry's running costs. So solar power is being tested as an aid to charge batteries for electric motors that can spin the propellers.

"Seemed like a good idea..."

Ship ferries have tried to carry railway trains across channels too wide for bridges. But uncoupling and loading the railroad cars took a long time. New tunneling technology means that tunnels are now usually the best answer.

New outrigger designs will give excellent stability even in rough seas, allowing ferries to keep to their strict schedules.

Proteus is a WAM-V, Wave-Adapted Modular Vessel. Its engines are in the two floatlike pontoons, and its flexible legs make sure the central pod has a smooth ride.

11

CARGO CARRIERS

More than nine-tenths of the world's cargo and traded goods go by sea. Craft that designers and engineers plan today will be in use for the next generation.

Quantum, *a design from DNV to carry 6,000 metal containers, will have plastic-composite materials to save weight, and a streamlined front windshield.*

New Drivers

Cargo ships are traditionally driven by fuel-thirsty marine diesel or turbine engines.

The hunt is on for new fuels and propulsion including hybrid electric-and-engine, gas-fuelled, and hydrogen fuel cells. There will also be help from solar power, computer-controlled sails, and even kites!

E-Ship 1 *carried its first cargo in 2010. Its four 89-foot (27-m) tall cylinders, called Flettner rotors, are spun around to help it to move forward more easily. This reduces fuel needs by one-third at its cruising speed of 18 miles per hour (29 km/h).*

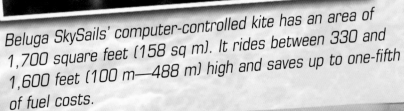

Beluga SkySails' computer-controlled kite has an area of 1,700 square feet (158 sq m). It rides between 330 and 1,600 feet (100 m—488 m) high and saves up to one-fifth of fuel costs.

Time is Money

For commercial carriers on short trips, time in the dock or port, loading and unloading, costs huge amounts of money. New methods include powerful magnets on cranes to lift metal container boxes, and adjustable pallets used as bases for many different kinds of cargo.

Azimuth thrusters are propellers on pods that swivel left or right. They make a ship more maneuverable, wasting less energy than rudders.

With zero carbon emissions, the Orcelle from Wallenius Wilhelmsen could carry 10,000 autos.

"Seemed like a good idea..."

Savannah *was the first and only nuclear-powered cargo vessel. It could carry a load of 8,000 tons (7,257 t) and sixty passengers in luxury. After its first voyage in 1962* Savannah *performed well at sea. But precautions and risks with nuclear power meant it was retired in 1972.*

Narrow sloped-back upper bow

Ulstein X-Bow

The X-bow is like the normal narrow, sloping front or bow of a ship—but upside down. It can give a much smoother ride in rough waves and also reduce water resistance or drag, with more speed for less fuel.

Lower bow projects forward below waterline

13

Skimmers and Amphibians

The Boeing 929 Jetfoil was one of the most successful hydrofoils, especially as a fast ferry across sheltered bays and estuaries.

It takes huge amounts of energy to push a ship through water and waves. So why not skim just above? Hydrofoils and similar designs have seen mixed success. However, future versions may conquer their old difficulties.

Wave-Cutters

A typical hydrofoil has narrow, ski-like "wings" or foils on struts below the hull. As these move through water they produce a lift force, like a plane's wings in air. The force lifts the craft so only the foils are in the water. However the ride can be rough and unstable, and also noisy with bumps and vibrations.

Based in Hong Kong, TurboJET operate several TriCat ferries. This one is testing a new HYSUWAC foil design that could halve fuel costs.

Futuristic designer Guillermo Sureda-Burgos proposes a hydrofoil version of a family automobile combined with a business jet plane. The HSSC rises on an oval-shaped front foil with a propeller-carrying tail foil for propulsion and extra stability.

FLOATERS

Air-cushion craft or hovercraft ride on a downflow of high-pressure air. They are amphibious—able to move from water to land and back again. But they use huge amounts of fuel. Also they are awkward to steer in high winds and big waves. New thruster designs and computer controls may ease this problem.

"Seemed like a good idea…"

Giant hovercraft like the SR.N4 could carry thirty cars and 250 people, and speed across busy shipping routes. But the energy needed to raise such weights meant the fuel costs were massive.

Airlift's tough Pioneer Mk3 hovercraft seats twenty-five passengers and cruises at 40 miles per hour (64 km/h).

In twenty-five years' time a hybrid hovercraft and jetski could be the big personal transport success, skimming over roads, grass, rough ground, swamps, and water.

Yachts and Racers

Wind power is free. It drives many kinds of sailships, from luxury yachts to ocean racers and fun dinghies. It once propelled cargo vessels, too. But the risk of being becalmed and late meant engines took over. Can sail come back into fashion?

At 190 feet (58 m) long, the WHY motor yacht's hull is adapted from the ramform design, giving extra stability and a huge deck area.

Project GreenJet *is a planned 187-foot (57-m) yacht with multi-sails that one operator can adjust on a touch-screen, according to the wind.*

Sails Plus

To reduce fuel use, and with it problems such as global warming, we could see another Age of Sail. Boats will rely on sail when the wind blows. But they would also have auxiliary or back-up systems such as electric-motor propellers powered by solar panels.

Maltese Falcon *has three masts each with five sails that unfurl by motors. Computers detect wind speed, direction, and other conditions, and suggest sail use.*

The Bavaria Deep Blue 46 luxury motor yacht was developed using designs, materials, and technologies borrowed from its automobile parent company, BMW.

Speed Kings

Few thrills match crashing into waves in a big powerboat. But fuel and engine costs for these monsters rocket every year. New trends include fuel cells for electric propulsion, lighter materials, and better hull designs to lessen drag.

In 2008 Earthrace (below) took the round-the-world powerboat record, at sixty-one days—using plant-based sustainable biodiesel.

Sun deck

Spa

Helipad

Stowage holds

Wing bridge

Wave-piercing bow

ICON 725 Super Yacht

Motor yachts like the Sabdes ICON 725, at 238 feet (73 m) long, boast all the comforts you can imagine, from spa to cinema. Yet they also bristle with energy-saving and environment-friendly devices, including the latest design of a wave-piercing bow to save engine power.

"Eco-friendly" super-yacht Soliloquy is propelled by a mix of solar, wind, and hybrid engine. Its solar panels cover 6,450 square feet (600 sq. m).

Soliloquy's rigid solar sails lift automatically and are adjusted by computers.

Personal Watercraft

PWCs, Personal Water-Craft, are a growing business. They are not just for fun, tourism, leisure, competitions, and stunts. They could become hard workers, even life-savers.

Going Solo

As PWCs' power, range, comfort, and safety improve, they may take on more roles in travel and transport. They might be used for riding to work each day, carrying small supplies around islands and across channels, and even as mini-lifeboats to rescue people in trouble at sea.

Maritime Flight Dynamics' experimental SeaPhantom *has a "lifting body" hull design for stability, borrowed from high-speed aircraft.*

Gibbs Technology's Quadski (right) *is a jet ski that can change into a quad bike at the flick of a switch. The Worx C-Quester mini-sub (below) sets new comfort standards.*

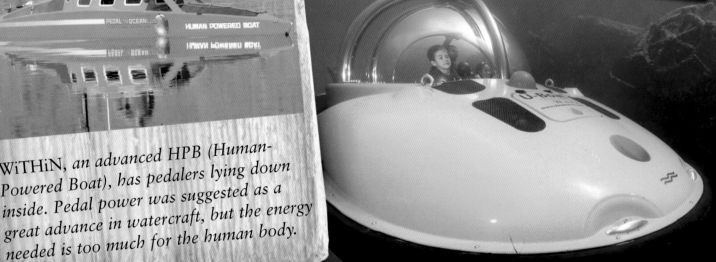

"Seemed like a good idea…"

WiTHiN, *an advanced HPB (Human-Powered Boat), has pedalers lying down inside. Pedal power was suggested as a great advance in watercraft, but the energy needed is too much for the human body.*

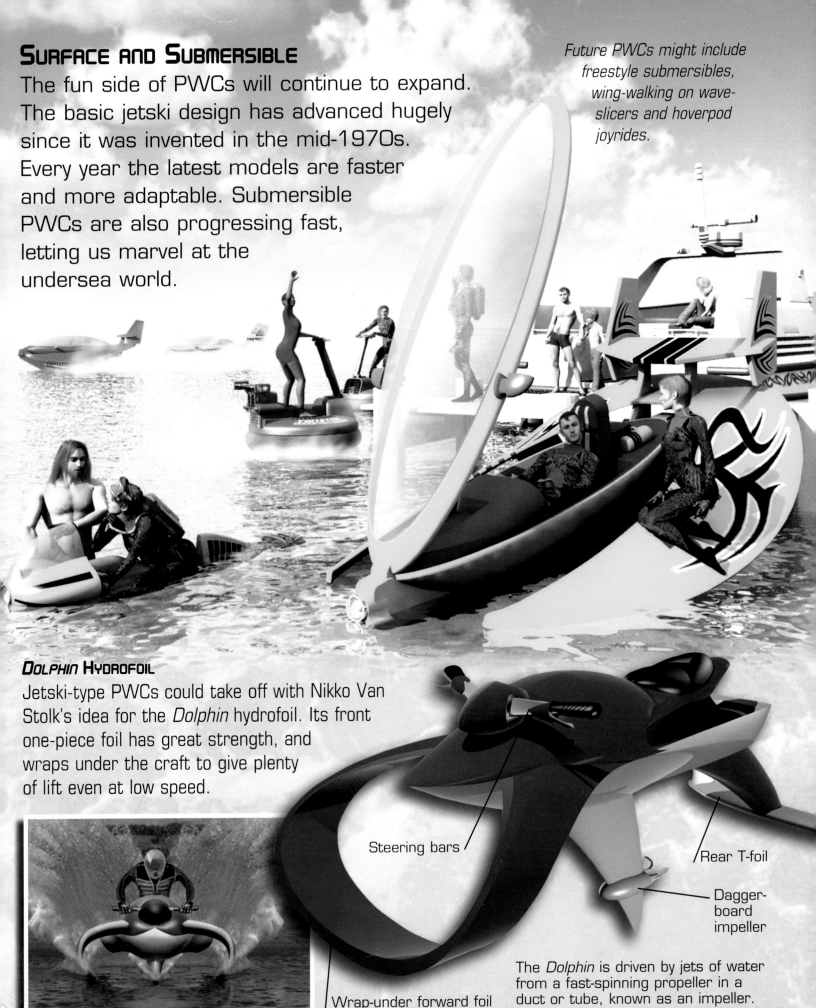

SURFACE AND SUBMERSIBLE

The fun side of PWCs will continue to expand. The basic jetski design has advanced hugely since it was invented in the mid-1970s. Every year the latest models are faster and more adaptable. Submersible PWCs are also progressing fast, letting us marvel at the undersea world.

Future PWCs might include freestyle submersibles, wing-walking on wave-slicers and hoverpod joyrides.

DOLPHIN HYDROFOIL

Jetski-type PWCs could take off with Nikko Van Stolk's idea for the *Dolphin* hydrofoil. Its front one-piece foil has great strength, and wraps under the craft to give plenty of lift even at low speed.

Steering bars

Rear T-foil

Dagger-board impeller

Wrap-under forward foil

The *Dolphin* is driven by jets of water from a fast-spinning propeller in a duct or tube, known as an impeller.

FUTURE NAVIES

Sea power founded great empires and forged trade links around the world. Next-generation navies will have to be fast, smart, and adaptable, as they respond to global needs.

Code-named Spearhead, TSV-1X (Theater Support Vessel) is a test U.S. Army support craft. Its trimaran design has two wave-piercer hulls.

SWATHs (Small Waterplane Area Twin Hulls) like Seafish resemble catamarans, but the two small, tube-shaped hulls stay under the surface.

Sea Superiority

The great battleships of the two World Wars were the deadliest weapons of their time. As air forces grew, navies also built supercarriers as floating air bases. The latest trends in warfare demand missile power, also sneaky stealth to avoid detection, and plenty of self-defence to repel enemy attack.

More than 1,000 feet (305 m) long, the U.S.'s Gerald R. Ford class of nuclear-powered supercarriers will carry seventy-five aircraft and hundreds of missiles.

"Seemed like a good idea..."

In 1874 Russian battleship Novograd was supposed to change naval warfare. Circular for stability, it could spin around to fire in any direction—but it was almost impossible to steer straight.

FLEXIBLE FIGHTERS

Forthcoming warships will probably be faster and also more flexible. They may need to switch roles—from a sudden dash to spy on suspicious events, to secret pursuit of a possible foe, to unleashing decisive firepower in the final battle.

The military hovercraft LCAC carries fighting vehicles, from jeeps to tanks, from oceangoing cargo carriers moored near the coast, through the shallows onto the shore.

The new U.S. Independence class warships have container-like modules fitted for different tasks.

STEALTH SHIPS

Stealth involves staying undetected by radar using shapes, surfaces and materials that scatter or absorb radar's radio waves. Engine noise, vibrations, and heat must also be much reduced.

Retractable gun turret inside hull

Radar-scattering angles

Future stealth warships like the U.S.'s planned Zumwalt class (above) are being designed with experience gained from existing vessels, such as Sweden's Visby class of small, light corvettes (right).

SUBMARINES AND SUBMERSIBLES

Beneath the surface, away from the wind, sun, and waves, it is calm and peaceful. This shadowy realm could be the next great highway for freight transport and perhaps people, either at work or enjoying the view.

Alvin the submersible has been making notable dives since the 1960s. It found a sunken atomic bomb in 1966, discovered deep-sea black smokers in 1977, and checked out sunken liner Titanic in 1986.

Britain's next-generation Astute class naval submarines went into service in 2010. With a crew of 100 and 323 feet (98 m) long, they carry thirty-eight torpedoes and missiles.

DIVERSE DIVERS

Submarines are larger craft that can undertake long voyages—some naval nuclear-powered subs stay underwater for months. Submersibles are smaller, go on shorter dives, and operate from a local port or a mother ship. Some stay near the surface, some dive down 4 miles (6.4 km)!

The Marion Hyper-Sub is a hybrid of fast powerboat on the surface, achieving 45 miles per hour (72 km/h), and go-anywhere, tough submersible.

U-Boat Worx's new C-Explorer 5 seats up to six people with an all-around view. It will be used for sightseeing, surveys, searches, and perhaps undersea rescue work.

Aqua-Bots

The future of underwater exploration and bulk transport may lie with remote-controlled underwater vehicles, ROVs. They do not need an air-filled, climate-controlled crew cabin, so their technology is much simplified.

ROV Hercules dives down 4 miles (6.4 km) on its connecting cable or tether. One of its grab arms is force-sensitive, meaning the human operator at the surface "feels" the hardness of objects it picks up.

"Seemed like a good idea..."

In 1775, U.S. patriot David Bushnell built his sub Turtle to attach explosives to British ships in the War of Independence. But all of Turtle's missions failed, and finally it sank.

Smaller roving submersibles (below left) may scout an area, before larger collecting craft (below right) arrive to gather mineral-rich rocks such as gold ore.

TRITON

RESCUE AND SURVIVAL

Accidents happen, especially out on the water. Breakdowns, storms, and rocky reefs are all hazards to shipping. Future rescue craft will brave all kinds of conditions to save lives and recover valuables.

On a life raft, water is all around—but salty and undrinkable. In this idea the Sun's rays evaporate seawater, condensing it to fresh.

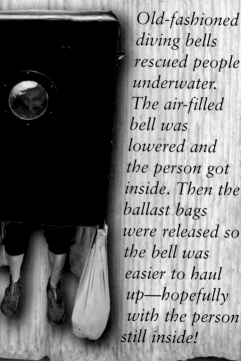

"Seemed like a good idea..."

Old-fashioned diving bells rescued people underwater. The air-filled bell was lowered and the person got inside. Then the ballast bags were released so the bell was easier to haul up—hopefully with the person still inside!

LIFEBOATS

The first big organized lifeboat service was the UK's Royal National Lifeboat Institution, way back in 1824. Other countries soon followed, such as the U.S. Coast Guard, USCG. One of the greatest advances was the self-righting design which turns right side up if knocked over.

The latest RNLI lifeboats (above) feature powerful diesel engines and all-weather protection. Planned USCG Sentinel fast-response cutters (left) will be able to stay at sea for five days.

LIFE RAFTS AND LIFE JACKETS

Safety demands that craft carry life jackets and/or life rafts for everyone aboard. Radio beacons may become standard even for individual life jackets. Thirst is a major survival problem, so jackets could have personal desalinators to take salt out of seawater.

Airboats with a catamaran hull design, and an airscrew or propeller for thrust, are ideal for shallow water work.

Inshore hovercraft skim over swamps and rocky shallows where lifeboats would founder.

Reaching the rescue zone fast is vital, before waves sweep stranded sailors to their doom. Future superspeed lifeboats could use ideas from offshore powerboat racers.

MARITIME TECH

As watercraft themselves improve in the future, so will their equipment, such as navigation, sonar, engines, and the way they power through the water.

The Cospas-Sarsat System uses eleven space satellites (left) that constantly listen for radio signals from radio distress beacons or EPIRBs (right). These are carried by ships and boats, as well as similar types in aircraft.

NAVIGATION

Progress in coming years should include fitting all ships and survival craft with better, more reliable distress radio beacons, also called EPIRBs (Emergency Position-Indicating Radio Beacons). This allows rescuers to pinpoint a position even in the middle of the ocean or hidden among cliffs on a remote coast.

"Seemed like a good idea..."

In 1845 the British warship Rattler (left), *with its newly invented propeller (screw), had a tug-of-war with paddle wheel-driven* Alecto. Rattler *won and paddlewheels quickly faded away.*

The U.S.'s newest RBM design, Response Boat Medium, has a twin-chine hull—a double ridge running from front to back. This greatly improves handling in heavy weather.

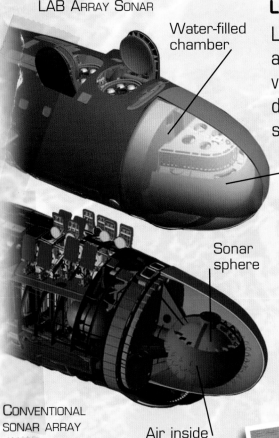

LAB ARRAY SONAR

Water-filled chamber

Bow array

Sonar sphere

CONVENTIONAL SONAR ARRAY

Air inside sphere

LARGE-APERTURE BOW [LAB] ARRAY SONAR

LAB array sonar "listens" for sound vibrations using a wrap-around device like a lens that collects and concentrates the vibrations. These are converted into electrical signals for display on the sonar screen.

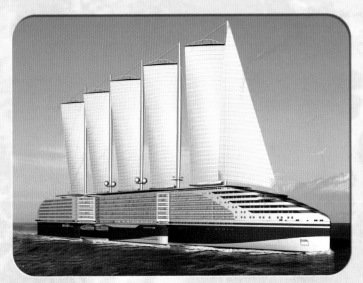

Sails that rise automatically in suitable winds, so the engines can slow or stop, are predicted as the next big trend in propulsion.

Tugboats work in crowded ports where pollution can be a problem. Electric tugs are a clean alternative and can recharge batteries overnight.

PROPULSION

Most ships are pushed along by propellers or waterscrews, and prop design is changing. The latest computer models show how the blade shape moves the water, so engineers can make tiny changes to give great increases in speed yet also save fuel.

Kort nozzles are collarlike shrouds or ducts around propellers. Their shape makes the water flow more smoothly for greater thrust.

FUTURE PORTS

As water transport advances, harbors and ports will become busier and more important. They will need better, faster links by road, rail, and air, as well as round-the-clock services.

SUPER SHELTERS

Ports vary from small island harbors to big leisure marinas, transport hubs for workers, and huge modern freight terminals. In years to come, automatic submersibles may patrol the sea lanes and tie-up berths. They will check for obstructions, and monitor vessels and water depth, sending in robot dredgers to carry away mud and sand.

Changing levels may be simple with the ship hoist. Like an extra-high lock, it lifts or lowers craft in a trough-shaped container, between the sea and the local canal network.

This Lilypad concept is an idea for a future floating city of 50,000 people, growing their own food and being self-sufficient in energy.

Ports will become even greater magnets for skyscrapers, stores, and apartments.

Port buildings have some of the world's most advanced designs. The planned headquarters for Antwerp, Belgium, have a new glass hull-shaped structure above the existing firefighters' building.

GYRE SEASCRAPER

Zigloo proposes a seascraper (rather than a land-based skyscraper) about as high as the Empire State Building, New York. Energy needs for the 2,000 inhabitants come from wind, tides, currents, and solar power.

"Seemed like a good idea..."

Over the years there have been several proposals for a floating port—in effect, a giant ship that acts as a safe harbor and refueling stop for smaller boats. This version from Japan dates back to the 1930s. But the costs would be colossal.

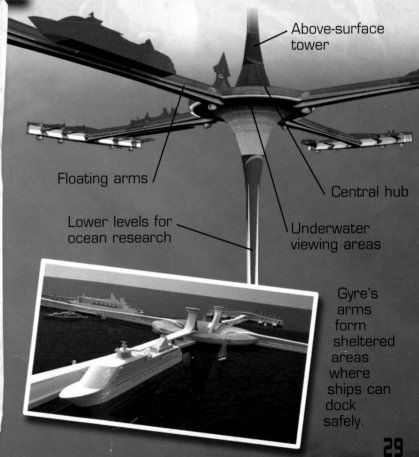

Above-surface tower

Floating arms

Central hub

Lower levels for ocean research

Underwater viewing areas

Gyre's arms form sheltered areas where ships can dock safely.

LOOK FURTHER!

Science predicts global warming and rising sea levels, so water transport and travel will become more common. Exciting new crafts and vessels will be less polluting, more energy-efficient, safer, and easier to use. The future world will be a wetter place!

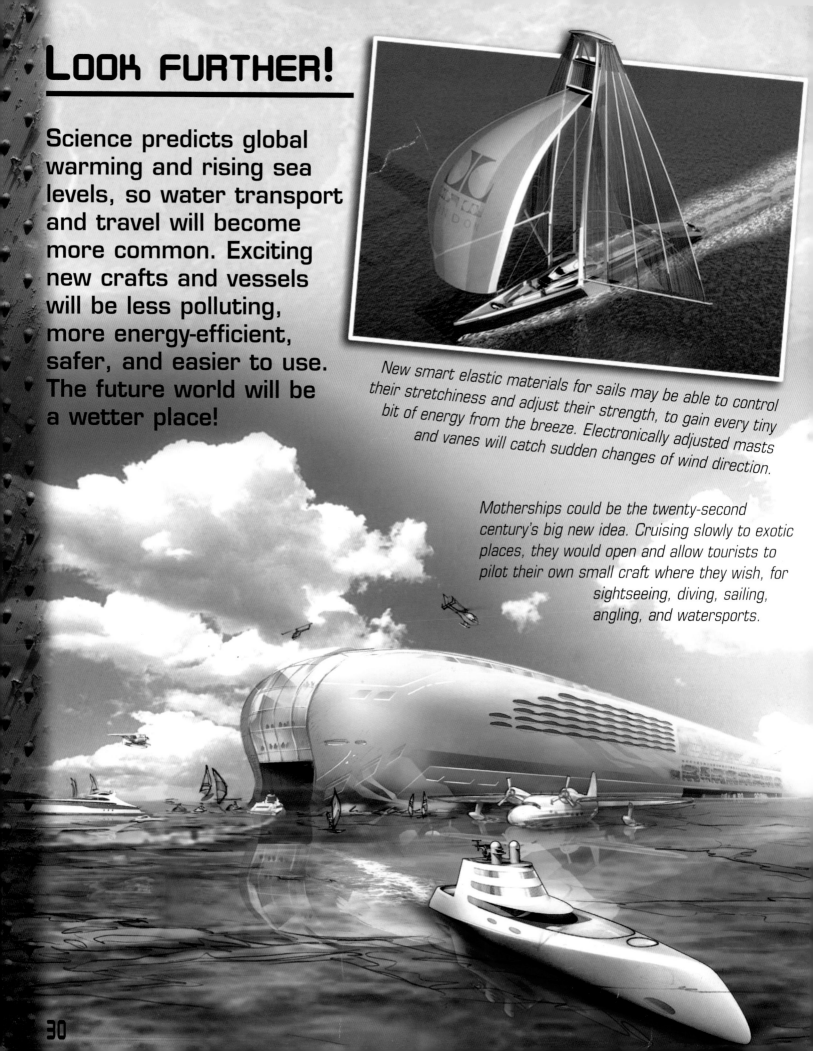

New smart elastic materials for sails may be able to control their stretchiness and adjust their strength, to gain every tiny bit of energy from the breeze. Electronically adjusted masts and vanes will catch sudden changes of wind direction.

Motherships could be the twenty-second century's big new idea. Cruising slowly to exotic places, they would open and allow tourists to pilot their own small craft where they wish, for sightseeing, diving, sailing, angling, and watersports.

Glossary

Azimuth thruster
A propeller or rotor in a pod or shroud that can swivel left or right, to change its direction of force and make a watercraft move sideways.

Composites
Materials made from several substances like plastics, carbon or glass fibers, resins, and ceramics.

Drag
Resistance in water or air—the force that slows any object trying to push past the tiny atoms and molecules of these substances.

Flettner Rotor
A tall tube or cylinder that spins and produces a force which can be used to propel watercraft or even aircraft.

Fuel Cell
A device that makes electricity from fuel such as hydrogen by splitting its atoms apart. It produces water as the main by-product.

Hybrid
A vehicle or craft with two or more forms of propulsion, such as an electric motor and sails for wind.

Impeller
A fast-spinning propeller or rotor in a tube or collarlike duct, or shroud, to make liquid flow through forcefully.

Lift
The force that pushes a craft up, usually from the "aerofoil" shape of airplane wings or water hydrofoils, which have a more curved upper surface than lower surface.

RoRo
Roll on, Roll off. A term used for ferries and other craft where wheeled vehicles can load and unload easily, without using equipment such as cranes or elevators.

Solar Cells and Panels
Button-sized electronic devices that turn light into electrical energy. Many solar cells in one large sheet are a solar panel (solar array).

Turbine
A rotating shaft with angled fan-shaped blades or rotors, which spin around when gases or liquids flow past them, or which turn to move a gas or liquid past them.

Index